CLIMATE CHANGE IMPACT
Air and Water Quality

Stuart A. Kallen

San Diego, CA

About the Author

Stuart A. Kallen is the author of more than 350 nonfiction books for children and young adults. He has written on topics ranging from the theory of relativity to the art of electronic dance music. In 2018 Kallen won a Green Earth Book Award from the Nature Generation environmental organization for his book *Trashing the Planet: Examining the Global Garbage Glut*. In his spare time he is a singer, songwriter, and guitarist in San Diego.

© 2025 ReferencePoint Press, Inc.
Printed in the United States

For more information, contact:
ReferencePoint Press, Inc.
PO Box 27779
San Diego, CA 92198
www.ReferencePointPress.com

ALL RIGHTS RESERVED.
No part of this work covered by the copyright hereon may be reproduced or used in any form or by any means—graphic, electronic, or mechanical, including photocopying, recording, taping, web distribution, or information storage retrieval systems—without the written permission of the publisher.

Picture Credits:

Cover: Black Sheep Media/Shutterstock.com

5: Dave Jonasen/Shutterstock.com
8: Jarek Kilian/Shutterstock.com
11: Arterra Picture Libary/Alamy Stock Photo
15: sruilk/Shutterstock.com
18: CHINE NOUVELLE/SIPA/Newscom
20: Christian Mueller/Shutterstock.com
25: ThirtyPlus/Shutterstock.com
28: APFootage/Alamy Stock Photo
32: LenaKing/Shutterstock.com
35: Tribune Content Agency LLC/Alamy Stock Photo
37: Geoffrey Clowes/Shutterstock.com
40: chayanuphol/Shutterstock.com
44: Greg Amptman/Shutterstock.com
48: Robin Loznak/Zuma Press/Newscom
50: Orjan Ellingvag/Alamy Stock Photo
54: Linda Rosier/Alamy Stock Photo

LIBRARY OF CONGRESS CATALOGING-IN-PUBLICATION DATA

Names: Kallen, Stuart A., 1955- author.
Title: Climate change impact: air and water quality / by Stuart A. Kallen.
Description: San Diego, CA : ReferencePoint Press, [2024] | Series: Climate change impact | Includes bibliographical references and index.
Identifiers: LCCN 2023048414 (print) | LCCN 2023048415 (ebook) | ISBN 9781678207786 (library binding) | ISBN 9781678207793 (ebook)
Subjects: LCSH: Climatic changes--Environmental aspects--Juvenile literature. | Water--Pollution--Juvenile literature. | Air--Pollution--Juvenile literature.
Classification: LCC HD75.6 .K35 2024 (print) | LCC HD75.6 (ebook) | DDC 333.7--dc23/eng/20231116
LC record available at https://lccn.loc.gov/2023048414
LC ebook record available at https://lccn.loc.gov/2023048415

CONTENTS

Introduction   **4**
The Planet Is Boiling

Chapter One   **7**
Gasping for Breath on a Hot Planet

Chapter Two   **17**
Smoke in the Air

Chapter Three   **27**
Watershed Woes

Chapter Four   **36**
Altered Oceans

Chapter Five   **46**
Solutions to Climate Pollution

Source Notes   56
Organizations and Websites   59
For Further Research   60
Index   61

INTRODUCTION

The Planet Is Boiling

In July 2023 doctor Joel Charles wrote, "Climate change is killing us."[1] Charles was referring to the heavy air pollution hitting his community in rural Wisconsin. The choking smoke was a result of the massive wildfires in Canada. For two weeks those same fires created pungent, eye-watering air pollution in Milwaukee, Chicago, and other midwestern states. Even short-term exposure to heavily polluted air can cause health problems, as Charles explains: "I have watched our vulnerable patients get sick from this smoke. . . . There is no safe level of exposure. . . . Air pollution contributes to preterm birth, stillbirths, delayed cognitive development in children, asthma, COPD [chronic obstructive pulmonary disease], heart disease, cancer, and dementia. When you do the work I do, you know those are real impacts, on real people."[2]

Children breathe faster than adults, inhaling two to three times more air. With lungs that are still developing, children are much more susceptible to air pollution. Thick smoke in the air makes kids more likely to develop respiratory problems later in life. And the respiratory system is only one part of the body affected by smoke. A 2015 study by the *Journal of the American Heart Association* showed that emergency room visits for heart attacks increased 42 percent within a day of exposure to wildfire smoke.

Wildfire peril does not dissipate after the flames are extinguished. The ashes, debris, sediment, and hazardous chemicals that are left behind wash into waterways. This toxic mixture fouls groundwater, drinking water, and aquatic environments. Water treatment engineer Monica Emelko understands the difficulty of providing clean drinking water to wildfire survivors when they return home after a disaster. After a wildfire devastated the city of Fort McMurray in Alberta, Canada, in 2016, Emelko says she saw poisonous sludge the color of hot fudge washing into the town water supply. "Fires are particularly hard on water," says Emelko. "If the intensity is there and enough of the watershed is burned, you can have a very significant impact on the water supply and that impact can be long-lasting."[3]

Climate Change Is to Blame

The 2023 Canadian wildfires occurred during the hottest year ever recorded on earth. And the sizzling summer temperatures drove extreme weather events that lowered air and water quality across the United States. Texas temperatures intensified asthma-inducing ozone air pollution, often referred to as smog. New England was hit by a series of unprecedented rainstorms. The subsequent flooding flushed untreated sewage, industrial waste, and other noxious substances into the rivers, lakes, and streams that people depend on for drinking water.

In 2023, smoke from wildfires in Canada obscured the Chicago skyline for days.

The World Weather Attribution group works with climate scientists to analyze weather events. The group said the extreme weather that increased air and water pollution in the United States, Canada, and elsewhere in 2023 would not have been possible without human-caused climate change. With temperatures soaring, dangerous fires and floods have become the norm. United Nations secretary-general António Guterres warns, "The era of global warming has ended; the era of global boiling has arrived."[4]

> ## CONSIDER THIS
>
> Exposure to wildfire smoke can worsen respiratory illnesses, including asthma, chronic obstructive pulmonary disease, and bronchitis.
>
> —US Environmental Protection Agency

Although critical to survival, clean air and healthy waterways are being challenged as never before. In 2023 more than 100 million people in the United States (or about one-third of the population) lived in areas with bad air quality, according to the US Environmental Protection Agency (EPA). And more than half the tap water in the United States is contaminated with chemicals that are considered dangerous to human health, according to the National Institutes of Health. Heat waves, floods, fires, and other severe weather events driven by climate change are expected to make air and water quality worse.

For nearly fifty years climate scientists have been warning that air and water quality, along with the health of the entire planet, is being dramatically altered due to the burning of coal, oil, and natural gas. Some individuals and groups are taking steps to fight climate change. Activists are protesting to change government policies that favor fossil fuel consumption. At the same time, a record number of electric cars, solar panels, wind turbines, and other technologies aimed at slowing climate change are being produced. These actions offer some hope, but much, much more will need to be done to fight the effects of climate change on air and water.

CHAPTER ONE

Gasping for Breath on a Hot Planet

Ella Roberta Kissi-Debrah was a playful, happy child growing up. Born in 2004 in London, she was a voracious reader by the age of seven and loved playing soccer, dancing, and making music. But in 2011 Ella Roberta got sick. She developed a persistent cough and chest infection and was soon disabled by chronic asthma. This led to over thirty visits to the hospital emergency room. In 2013 Ella Roberta's life was cut short by a fatal asthma attack a few months after her ninth birthday.

Acute respiratory failure was listed as the official cause of Ella Roberta's death. Her mother, Rosamund, believes that Ella Roberta was killed by air pollution caused by heavy vehicle traffic in her South East London neighborhood. Rosamund hired a lawyer who worked for years to arrange a new investigation into Ella Roberta's death. In 2020 a second inquest was conducted by coroner Philip Barlow, who concluded, "Air pollution was a significant contributory factor to both the induction and exacerbations of her asthma. . . . Ella died of asthma contributed to by exposure to excessive air pollution."[5] The coroner's finding led to a change on the girl's death certificate. In December 2020 she became the first person in the world to have air pollution listed as her official cause of death.

Hot Air and Smog

The main pollutants that caused Ella Roberta's death were listed as nitrogen dioxide (NO_2) and particulate matter. These pollutants are produced by cars, trucks, buses, power plants, and some industrial facilities. The type of air pollution that made Ella Roberta fatally ill has been common for more than a century. But the harmful effects of NO_2 and particulate matter are increasing as climate change continues to impact air quality.

During normal weather conditions, air pollution rises into the atmosphere, where it is dispersed by winds. When heat waves occur, high pressure in the atmosphere pushes warm air—and air pollution—down to the ground. The sinking air acts as a cap, called a heat dome, that traps the heat already on the ground. Heat domes push away cooling winds and shade-giving clouds. As geoscience professor Gabriel A. Vecchi explains, "Basically we just get the sun pouring down sunshine unimpeded, baking the ground, and no real cloud cover or moisture to stave off our temperatures."[6] When the air becomes stagnant, sunlight reacts with NO_2 and other air pollutants to produce ground-level ozone. Commonly referred to as smog, ground-level ozone creates a brown haze that hangs over most big cities, especially in the summer. Smog is a powerful lung irritant that can trigger asthma attacks and other lung diseases.

The harmful effects of NO_2 and particulate matter produced by cars are increasing climate change.

The ill effects of air pollution were described in *The Health Argument for Climate Action*, published by the World Health Organization (WHO) in 2021. The guide is dedicated to the memory of Ella Roberta Kissi-Debrah "and all other children who have suffered and died from air pollution and climate change."[7] The WHO report points out that while Ella Roberta was the first to have her death officially attributed to air pollution, bad air kills over 8 million people worldwide every year. Millions more suffer from the debilitating effects of heart and respiratory diseases caused by air pollution.

> ## CONSIDER THIS
>
> In the United States nearly 120 million people were exposed to unhealthy levels of soot and smog in 2023.
>
> —American Lung Association

Black Carbon

The WHO report highlights a climate pollutant known as black carbon. Black carbon, commonly called soot, is generated by burning fossil fuels. The main sources of black carbon are coal-fired power plants and diesel engines. Black carbon is also known as fine particulate matter or particle pollution. The particles are in a category of airborne pollutants known as PM2.5. This designation indicates that the particles have a diameter of 2.5 micrometers or less. By comparison, a grain of fine beach sand is around 90 micrometers. Because of their tiny size, black carbon particles can easily enter the body.

The average person takes around twenty thousand breaths every day. Air enters the lungs, where blood cells pick it up, and travel through the bloodstream to deliver oxygen to the muscles, heart, brain, and other systems. When people inhale larger particles like dust and sand, they cough to expel the material from the lungs. But fine particle pollution gets absorbed by the lungs, as Paul Billings of the American Lung Association explains: "The small particles get down deep and they get into the bloodstream and cause a wide range of adverse health effects. Coughing, wheezing. Shortness of breath. They've also been linked to lung cancer, heart attack, stroke and thousands and thousands of premature deaths."[8]

A 2022 study by the WHO determined that particulate pollution contributes to 6.7 million premature deaths worldwide every year, with about 110,000 of those deaths in the United States.

In addition to harming human health, black carbon is contributing to climate change. The WHO classifies black carbon as a short-lived climate pollutant. While carbon dioxide (CO_2), the main driver of climate change, remains in the air for centuries, black carbon only remains in the atmosphere for around ten days. The problem is that black carbon absorbs sunlight and converts it into heat. This gives the substance a warming impact up to fifteen hundred times stronger than CO_2. United Nations environmental correspondent Niklas Hagelberg explains how black carbon contributes to climate change: "Air pollution in the form of particulate matter from diesel engines is circulated around the globe, ending up in the most remote places, including the polar regions.

Environmental Injustice

The combination of record-setting heat and air pollution takes a toll on almost everyone who has to endure these twin problems of climate change. But numerous studies in the United States have shown that people of color and those with low incomes suffer more than those who live in wealthier, White-majority neighborhoods. Black-majority neighborhoods are more likely to be located near heavily polluting freeways, refineries, factories, and power plants. Lower-income neighborhoods with significantly fewer parks, trees, and green spaces can be up to 6°F (3.4°C) hotter during heat waves, according to satellite data compiled by University of California researchers. It is also harder for Black Americans to escape the heat and pollution on sweltering days. A 2020 study of Black-majority neighborhoods in South Los Angeles showed that three-fifths of the households did not have air-conditioning.

According to the Centers for Disease Control and Prevention, Black Americans inhale 56 percent more particulate matter than they produce by their own consumption. This contrasts with White people who inhale 17 percent less particulate matter than is caused by their consumption. This is one of the reasons that Black people are 30 percent more likely than White people to have asthma. And Black children are nearly eight times more likely to die from asthma-related causes than White children.

The Falljökull glacier in Iceland (pictured) is blackened from deposits of carbon and soot.

When it lands on ice and snow it darkens them slightly, leading to less sunlight being reflected back into space, and contributing to global warming."[9]

The Feedback Loop

Hagelberg calls air pollution and climate change two sides of the same coin. What he means is that climate change can lower air quality, and conversely, bad air quality can worsen climate change. This is what has come to be known as a feedback loop. Another example of a feedback loop can be seen in the widespread use of air conditioners as climate change increases the number of days with excessive heat. Air conditioners are power-hungry machines that use more electricity than other household appliances. According to Silicon Valley Power, a single-room air conditioner uses as much energy per hour as four refrigerators or twenty-three large-screen televisions.

To keep up with demand, power plants have to generate more electricity. During this process, power plants that rely on coal, oil, and natural gas pump more pollutants—including black

CONSIDER THIS

Rising temperatures since 1970 have led to longer allergy seasons in over 170 cities across the United States.

—Climate Central

carbon, NO_2, and CO_2—into the air. During a record-setting heat wave in China in 2022, 50 percent of all electricity being generated was used to run air conditioners. While China is working to double its wind and solar energy capacity, nearly two-thirds of the nation's power plants are fueled by coal. This further aggravates the problem of climate change. A headline in *Science* magazine succinctly defined the climate change feedback loop: "The Hotter It Gets, the Hotter It Gets."

The feedback loop is expected to accelerate as the planet continues to warm and the number of air conditioners increases. According to the International Energy Agency, there were around 1.2 billion air-conditioning units worldwide in 2023. By 2050 that number is expected to increase to 4.5 billion. The Natural Resources Defense Council crunched those numbers and concluded that the increased energy demand from air-conditioning and other cooling measures will increase ground-level smog by 16 percent and particulate matter by around 60 percent above current levels. This will also worsen climate change, producing an extra 2.2 billion tons (2 billion metric tonnes) of CO_2 annually.

The World Meteorological Organization (WMO) says this interaction between air pollution and climate change imposes a "climate penalty" on hundreds of millions of people. This penalty is explained by WMO secretary-general Petteri Taalas: "As the globe warms . . . air pollution [is] expected to increase, even under a low emissions scenario. In addition to human health impacts, this will also affect ecosystems as air pollutants settle from the atmosphere to Earth's surface. We have seen this in the heatwaves in Europe and China [in 2022] when . . . sunlight and low wind speeds were conducive to high pollution levels."[10]

Plant Problems

There is no longer any doubt that the planet is warming. Scientists say human-made climate change has caused average global temperatures to rise 2°F (1°C) in the past two centuries. While two degrees does not sound like much, the rising temperatures have upset the balance of nature. Warmer temperatures are causing catastrophic fires, floods, droughts, and other extreme weather. The world is not currently on track to limit global warming, and some scientists predict average world temperatures will rise by more than 7°F (4°C) by 2100.

These higher temperatures could further harm air quality in unexpected ways. A 2023 study by the University of California, Riverside (UCR), showed that the temperature changes could cause plants to release harmful pollutants into the air. All plants naturally emit small amounts of chemicals known as biogenic volatile organic compounds, or BVOCs. These emissions are gener-

Desert Dust

The world's largest desert, the Sahara in North Africa, is getting bigger due to climate change. This desert expansion is producing massive dust clouds that increase air pollution when carried west by the winds. In 2020 a huge dust plume from the Sahara traveled over the Atlantic Ocean more than 2,000 miles (3,219 km) to the Caribbean and the United States. While Saharan dust clouds are an annual phenomenon, the 2020 event was the most intense on record. Millions of people in Miami, Houston, New Orleans, and elsewhere were warned to stay indoors as a shadowy brown haze of dust triggered air quality alerts throughout the South. Witnesses say the extremely large dust storm turned day into night as it passed overhead.

Saharan dust is made up of a type of pollution called fine particulate matter. James Gomez, a researcher at the University of California, Riverside, expects dust storms like this to increase in number, size, and density as average global temperatures soar. "We are causing these changes in the natural system," Gomez says. "Nature is making the air pollution worse, as a result of our net actions."

Quoted in Angely Mercado, "An Unexpected Reason It'll Be Harder to Breathe as Earth Warms," Gizmodo, March 3, 2023. https://gizmodo.com.

ally not harmful because they are produced in very small quantities. In fact, plants are an important buffer against climate change despite producing BVOCs because they remove CO_2 from the air and produce oxygen.

However, rising CO_2 levels coupled with hotter temperatures can cause plants to produce higher levels of BVOCs. When that happens, the compounds react with oxygen to produce aerosols, or tiny liquid droplets suspended in air. The aerosols are classified as fine particulate matter, or PM2.5. BVOC aerosols have been linked to infant deaths and asthma. In adults the compounds can cause lung cancer and heart disease.

> **CONSIDER THIS**
>
> In Delhi, India, air pollution is estimated to reduce average life expectancies by nine years.
>
> —University of Chicago Air Quality Life Index

According to the UCR report, about two-thirds of future pollution is predicted to come just from plants. James Gomez, lead author of the study, says an increase in BVOCs could create a new public health hazard: "Really anybody that has respiratory issues could be negatively impacted by [BVOC] air pollution. Even an average healthy person who breathes in excessive amounts of air pollution could be negatively affected and develop respiratory issues."[11]

Pollen and Allergies

Higher CO_2 levels and rising temperatures are affecting plants in other ways that impact public health. Warm weather provides a signal to plants to produce flowers that release pollen into the air. This is a source of misery every spring and summer for around 81 million Americans with seasonal allergies, who experience coughing, sneezing, itchy eyes, runny noses, and other symptoms caused by pollen from trees, grass, weeds, and other plants. Their suffering is compounded by climate change. Warmer winters are causing spring to arrive earlier. As a result of this change, the length of allergy season has increased by about twenty days on average since 1990, according to the National Academy of Sciences.

Spruce branches release pollen. Pollen spores can easily enter the lungs and cause allergies.

Climate change is also causing plants to produce more sneeze-inducing pollen. William Anderegg, a University of Utah professor who studies climate change and seasonal allergies, estimates that pollen concentrations have increased 20 percent in the past thirty years. This is due to more CO_2 in the atmosphere, which causes flowers to grow bigger and produce more pollen per flower.

Plant pollen is not considered air pollution. But pollen spores, much like black carbon, are fine particulate matter that can easily enter the lungs. Anderegg says seasonal allergies are especially harmful to children with asthma who live in places where air pollution is already a problem. According to Anderegg, worsening allergies are "a really clear example of how climate change is impacting us now, every spring, in every breath that we take. This is climate change in our own backyards, in our own towns and cities. It's not future generations or other countries or future decades."[12]

Two Problems: One Solution

In 2023 the WHO issued health-based recommendations for air quality for the first time in fifteen years. The WHO reports that an astonishing 99 percent of the global population breathes polluted air that exceeds its air quality guidelines, which determine safe exposure levels of various pollutants. The organization calls air pollution an invisible danger and notes that harm can be caused by breathing even low levels of fine particulate matter, ozone, nitrous oxide, sulfur dioxide, and other pollutants. The report also says fossil fuels are responsible for the most harmful emissions.

The WHO notes that cutting back on fossil fuel consumption would slow climate change. This in turn would improve air quality, which would lead to improved health for people around the world. Momentum on this front is growing. According to the WHO report, in 2012 around eleven hundred cities in 91 countries monitored air quality. And in 2022 more than six thousand cities in 117 countries monitored air quality. As millions more people come to understand what is in the air they are breathing—and the associated climate problems—measures can be taken to reduce the harm. As WHO director general Tedros Adhanom Ghebreyesus says, "The urgency of addressing the twin health challenges of air pollution and climate change underscore the pressing need to move faster towards a world that is much less dependent on fossil fuels."[13]

CHAPTER TWO

Smoke in the Air

The 2023 fire season in Canada was one for the record books. The first wildfires broke out in Quebec in late April. Within weeks more than forty fires were burning through the province's dense pine forests. In June, wildfires in the west were consuming thousands of acres of forest in British Columbia. By August more than one thousand wildfires were burning out of control in all ten Canadian provinces and the Northwest Territories. By September the fires had consumed more than 43.4 million acres (17.6 million ha). Canadian prime minister Justin Trudeau blamed the fires on record-setting heat, strong winds, and a years-long drought—all of which were made worse by climate change.

The Canadian conflagrations sent tremendous plumes of murky brown smoke into the air. The smoke was then carried south by prevailing winds. Along the East Coast of the United States and throughout the US Midwest, the summer of 2023 will be remembered as a time when the skies turned orange and choking smoke blotted out the sun. On June 27 the air quality in Chicago was worse than any other major city in the world. The air quality was nearly as poor in Milwaukee, Detroit, and other cities in the region. AirNow, a US government site that measures air quality, rated air quality across the Midwest as either unhealthy or very unhealthy.

Chicago doctor Ravi Kalhan is a pulmonologist, a doctor who specializes in respiratory conditions. Kalhan says breathing air that is rated as unhealthy or worse for a single day is equivalent to smoking half a pack of cigarettes. In healthy people, the wildfire smoke caused irritation of the eyes, nose, and throat, along with coughing, sneezing, and shortness of breath. For those with

The McDougall Creek wildfire burns in West Kelowna, British Columbia, in August 2023. Canada had a record fire season in 2023.

chronic heart and lung conditions, the unhealthy air meant visits to the emergency room. For some the pollution triggered fatal asthma and heart attacks. According to Kalhan, "If the frequency of those [unhealthy air] days increase[s] or if the exposure occurs when the person is younger, spends more time outdoors, then it probably has more long-term impacts on health and creates, you know, a true public health problem that we need to understand."[14]

Impacting Mental Health

The public health problems associated with breathing wildfire smoke extend beyond physical ailments. Exposure to fires and smoke can also threaten mental health, according to a study published in 2023 by a team of psychologists at Australia's University of New England. The research was conducted after Australia experienced nine months of record-setting fires in 2019 and 2020. Australians refer to this period as the Black Summer. By the time the Black Summer ran its course, over 46 million acres (18.6 million ha) had burned across Australia.

The smoke from the Black Summer wildfires was so thick that life ground to a halt in Sydney, Australia's largest city. Fire alarms were automatically triggered in office buildings, and shipping traffic was shut down in the city's harbor due to lack of visibility. Thirty-three people died and more than six thousand buildings were destroyed in what was then one of the largest wildfires of the twenty-first century.

After the Black Summer flames were extinguished, the University of New England psychologists interviewed nearly eight hundred people ages sixteen to twenty-five. The researchers found that those who were directly exposed to wildfire smoke experienced greater incidents of depression, anxiety, stress, and substance abuse. The young people also had increased levels of what the study defined as climate-change distress: "[Their futures were] impacted by climate change they did little to contribute to but from which they will suffer the longest-term effects. . . . They felt that the effects of climate change were more likely to affect them or people like them, to occur nearer to them geographically, and to happen sooner in time."[15]

> ## CONSIDER THIS
>
> **The amount of land burned in British Columbia, Canada, in 2023 was 5,000 percent above normal.**
>
> —Natural Resources Canada

The Australian study was among the first to look at the psychological effects of wildfires on young people. But other studies have linked attention-deficit/hyperactivity disorder and other mental problems in children to long-term exposure to any type of air pollution. And a 2022 study in China found that young people living in areas with high levels of air pollution had a nearly 30 percent higher risk of experiencing anxiety than those who live in less-polluted areas.

Chemical Compounds

Wildfire smoke is particularly hazardous to human health because it contains more than burning plant matter. When massive fires sweep through populated areas, the flames consume houses, stores, vehicles, garbage, and even roads. According to the EPA, when gas, oil, asphalt, and similar substances burn at high temperatures, the smoke contains hazardous air pollutants called polycyclic aromatic hydrocarbons (PAHs). There are about five hundred different toxic compounds classified as PAHs. The chemicals irritate the eyes and breathing passages. Long-term PAH exposure is associated with an increased risk of breast, lung, and other cancers.

Hundreds of other cancer-causing compounds are spread when building materials, synthetic fibers, home furnishings, electronics, agricultural chemicals, and other products burn. These toxins include chlorine, asbestos, and heavy metals such as lead, mercury, arsenic, and cadmium. As environmental health researcher Boya Zhang writes, "For wildfires, we only think about trees or grasslands burning. But [wildfires burn] everything in their path, including gas stations and houses, emitting some really toxic components."[16]

Building supplies are stacked at a construction site. When building materials burn in wildfires, they spread cancer-causing compounds.

The East Coast "Smoke-pocalypse"

When smoke from the Quebec wildfires blew into US cities from Portland, Maine, to Washington, DC, in June 2023, the sky turned an eerie orange-brown color. This created street scenes that resembled a postapocalyptic movie, causing the term *smoke-pocalypse* to go viral on social media. The smoke-polluted air forced restaurants and schools to close and professional sports leagues to delay games. Federal officials shut down East Coast air travel due to poor visibility, causing delays or cancellations of six hundred flights. In Washington, DC, the White House Gay Pride celebration, expected to attract thousands, had to be postponed. As the air began to clear in the Northeast, winds blew the smoke south and west, forcing eighteen states to issue air quality alerts.

Even after the smoke had cleared, the air still contained pollutants that could affect people's health. "I don't know if people understand how bad it can be," says University of California, Davis, researcher Keith Bein. Air pollutants from wildfires do not immediately go away even though the smoke has cleared, he explains. The pollution is "still in the air, it's still coming off your clothes and walls. The same is going to apply if it infiltrates your home and coats your walls, it doesn't disappear when the plume disappears."

Quoted in Dani Anguiano, "Surviving the Smoke-pocalypse 101: Californians Offer Advice to New Yorkers," *The Guardian* (Manchester, UK), June 8, 2023. www.theguardian.com.

Toxic Ash

Particle pollution is one of the main components of wildfire smoke. Harmful particle pollution is also produced by cars, factories, and power plants. But researchers have found that PM2.5 originating from wildfires can be three to four times more damaging to the lungs than other types of particulate pollution. That is because wildfire particles carry chemicals such as sulfuric acid, from cleaning agents and car batteries, and ammonium nitrate, found in fertilizers, explosives, and some refrigerants. The toxins that adhere to ashes and soot fall back to earth. When the wind blows, this polluted mix is propelled throughout the environment.

The particle pollution problems associated with wildfires could be seen in 2023 when fires swept across the island of Maui in the state of Hawaii. The fire almost completely destroyed the historic beach town of Lahaina, leaving thousands of residents homeless. More than ninety-five people died, making the Lahaina conflagration one of the deadliest US wildfires in the past century. When survivors returned to their homes to sort through the ashes, they were cautioned to cover themselves from head to toe and wear masks to avoid inhaling the toxic ash. Engineering professor Andrew Whelton issued a warning: "People are going back to their properties that may have destroyed structures and encountering hazards that could make them acutely sick if they're not protected."[17]

> ## CONSIDER THIS
>
> Nearly 90 percent of homeless people in Salt Lake County, Utah, sought medical attention for conditions associated with air pollution in 2020.
>
> —University of Utah

In 2023 researchers at the University of Michigan linked particle pollution to dementia, a devastating disease associated with extreme memory loss and reduced cognitive capacity. The study said exposure to fine particle pollution results in an estimated 188,000 dementia diagnoses each year. Zhang, who was the lead author of the study, said fine particle pollution caused by wildfires had the strongest links to dementia: "The main reason for this distinction may be due to the different physical or chemical characteristics of the PM2.5 from these different sources. All particles are harmful to you, but wildfires . . . may be more harmful to your cognitive health."[18]

Indoor Pollution

Dementia mostly occurs in people over fifty and can take years to develop. But air pollution from wildfires can cause immediate problems for those who suffer from asthma. This was seen on June 27, 2023, when wildfire smoke from Canada enveloped New York City. On that day, the air quality was classified for a time as very unhealthy or hazardous by New York governor Kathy Hochul. The deteriorating air quality on June 27 resulted in more emergency room visits for asthma-related problems than in all of 2023.

Homeless in Polluted Air

When wildfire smoke blows into urban population centers, public health officials warn people to stay indoors to prevent lung damage. But those who are homeless often have nowhere to go to escape the smoke. When Canadian wildfires caused Chicago to experience several days with the worst air quality in the world in the summer of 2023, volunteers handed out masks and water to people living in tents and under highway overpasses.

The air in Chicago and many other cities is often dangerously polluted even when wildfires are not burning. A 2022 study from the Cleveland Clinic found that around 60 percent of unhoused people spend most of their time next to roadways, where they are constantly exposed to particulate matter and other air pollutants. Researchers say the homeless are most affected by wildfires, even when they are burning thousands of miles away. According to Katie League, a behavioral health manager at the National Health Care for the Homeless Council, "With any natural disaster, we emphasize that people experiencing homelessness experience it first, they experience it worst, and they generally experience it longest."

Quoted in Siri Chilukuri, "How Air Pollution and the Housing Crisis Are Connected," *Grist*, July 7, 2023. https://grist.org.

The effects of the smoky air were felt more acutely in New York's Black-majority neighborhoods. For example, during the 2023 wildfires, asthma suffers from the Bronx made up 27 percent of the visits to emergency rooms while representing only 16 percent of the city's population. Researchers say the problem can be partially blamed on low-quality housing, which is most common in poor neighborhoods.

Most people spend 90 percent of their time indoors, according to the EPA. Outdoor air comes into a house or apartment through open doors and windows or through heating and cooling systems. In a process called infiltration, outdoor air also enters buildings through cracks around doors, windows, floors, ceilings, and roofs. These cracks, which are more common in poorly maintained buildings, allow smoke and particulates into living areas even when doors and windows are shut. As pulmonary physician Neeta Thakur says, "We talk about sheltering in place, but if your home, the place where you stay all the time, if it's an older building and hasn't been repaired, a lot of that wildfire smoke could be getting inside, and you are being exposed."[19]

Air conditioners and air purifiers can help offset some of the harm from indoor smoke pollution, but these appliances are too expensive for many low-income people. Most rely on window fans, which blow polluted air directly into the home. Making matters worse, the 2023 fires occurred during a heat wave. People went outdoors into the smoky air when the heat inside their houses or apartments became too much.

A Losing Combination

The combination of high temperatures and air pollution from wildfires is a major contributor to early death in the United States and elsewhere. According to Melissa Gonzales, chair of the Department of Environmental Health Sciences at Tulane University, "Individually, each one of these is hazardous. Put them together, and they're compounding the effects of one another."[20]

A 2022 study by the University of Southern California looked at deaths from respiratory and heart disease over a five-year period and how they were impacted by the twin problems of heat and air pollution. Researchers determined that the risk of early death rises 21 percent on days with both excessive heat and high levels of particulate matter. The study determined that if the body gets dehydrated due to extreme heat, blood vessels contract, or get smaller. This decreases the flow of oxygenated blood to tissues and organs. The heart beats faster to compensate, which can increase blood pressure to dangerous levels. This stress causes two major problems. People breathe harder, which makes them inhale more particulate matter. And when blood vessels constrict, the body loses its ability to rid itself of fine particulate matter and other pollutants. This can result in tissue and cell damage, increasing the risk of heart attacks and cancer.

The study noted that California has experienced a fivefold increase in wildfires since 1970 as global temperatures have increased due to climate change. According to the authors of the

When people breathe harder they inhale more particulate matter, and when blood vessels constrict, the body loses its ability to rid itself of pollutants like these, making a heart attack more likely.

study, "Short-term exposure to extreme heat and air pollution alone were individually associated with increased risk of mortality."[21] Exposure to both high heat and polluted air had an even greater effect on people's health.

Every Living Creature

Throughout 2023 more than 250 wildfires burned out of control in Canada. Around one-third of the US population—120 million people—was exposed to heavy wildfire smoke that drifted south. Low-lying smoke from Canadian fires was also detected in the United Kingdom, Portugal, France, Norway, and other European nations. Around the same time, parts of Europe were also experiencing extreme heat and wildfires. In the summer of 2023, the largest wildfires ever recorded in the European Union cut across Greece, Italy, and Spain's Canary Islands. Smoke from these fires drifted south across the Mediterranean Sea, darkening skies in North Africa.

Several studies published in 2023 exposed the depth of the problem. Australian researchers found that from 2010 to 2019 over 2 billion people worldwide were exposed to at least one day of fire-related air pollution. Research published in the journal *Nature* found that wildfires in the United States have eroded progress on cleaning up other sources of air pollution. Wildfires in Oregon and Nevada have been especially damaging to this effort. According to Marshall Burke, lead author of the study and professor of earth system science, "We had had so much success [cleaning up air pollution], and wildfires, just in five to six years, are really unraveling a lot of this progress."[22]

> ## CONSIDER THIS
>
> In 2023 people of color were 64 percent more likely than White people to breathe unhealthy air.
>
> —American Lung Association

Long-range smoke from wildfires is more than a people problem. Livestock, pets, and wild animals are also exposed to the unhealthful effects of wildfire smoke. As environmental studies professor Gail Carlson writes, "Air pollution is a major, major health threat, and that is true for anybody with lungs."[23]

Stephen J. Pyne, emeritus professor at Arizona State University, has studied the countless ways wildfires have harmed people while transforming the earth's natural landscape. Pyne's research has led him to state that humanity has entered a new epoch he calls the Pyrocene era. This era is marked by gargantuan wildfires linked to the climate-changing effects of burning fossil fuels. Pyne describes the Pyrocene era: "Places that have fire now are likely to experience it more frequently and more intensely. Places that have little fire now may acquire it, depending on how climatic shifts interact with what people do. . . . However the Pyrocene [era] evolves, we have a lot of fire in our future."[24]

CHAPTER THREE

Watershed Woes

In July 2023 Vermont was inundated by a record-breaking storm that dumped a month's worth of rain on the state in a single day. Catastrophic floods wiped out roads and bridges, created mudslides, and forced thousands of people from their homes. In Montpelier, the state capital, more than 9 inches (23 cm) of rain flooded the downtown area with thick, brown water that smelled of natural gas and sewage. The polluted water coated buildings, vehicles, and people struggling to evacuate to higher ground.

David Camley felt lucky. His apartment in Johnson, Vermont, about 35 miles (56 km) north of the capital, was one of the few that did not get flooded. But as the waters receded, he had another problem: Camley's residence reeked of No. 2 fuel oil, also known as heating oil, a petroleum product commonly used to fuel furnaces in New England. As Camley says, "I opened my door up and I tried to air it out some, cause I got a dog and she was getting sick from it. And me too, not sleeping, smelling that for three days."[25]

Camley's problems could be traced to a tank of fuel oil in his building that was overturned when the basement flooded. As a cleanup crew pumped the mess from the basement, hoses directed the water into a storm drain, which carried the toxic substance into the nearby Lamoille River. While Camley's problem was an isolated one, there were more than two hundred flood-related hazardous chemical spills in Vermont as a result of the storm. The rain and subsequent flooding washed unknown amounts of fuel oil, gasoline, and other toxins into rivers and lakes. Insecticides, herbicides, and fungicides flowed into waterways from agricultural lands, golf courses, lawns, and gardens. Additionally, the floodwaters overwhelmed

This is an aerial view of Montpellier, Vermont, in July 2023, when record-breaking storms caused catastrophic flooding.

at least twenty-four Vermont wastewater facilities, polluting waterways with raw sewage. Catastrophic rainstorms also hit parts of New York, New Hampshire, Massachusetts, and Connecticut, causing similar problems across the Eastern Seaboard.

Hot Air Holds More Water

According to the US government's National Climate Assessment, New England now receives an average of 55 percent more rain than it did in 1958. Basic climate change science is behind this trend. More than 70 percent of the planet is water. As fossil fuel consumption increases temperatures across the planet, more moisture from the oceans evaporates into the atmosphere. Warmer air holds more water; when it rains there is more precipitation in the clouds. This results in more intense rainfall events and destructive floods that collapse buildings, destroy infrastructure such as buildings and road, and drown people in their cars and homes.

Stronger downpours related to climate change were blamed for extreme rain and flooding in Kentucky and Illinois in 2023. Severe rain events and floods were also reported in Canada, Spain, India, and China. As water scientist Peter Gleick noted in July 2023, "The news in the last couple of months has just been relentless, nonstop, extreme events. It's everything, everywhere, all at once. It's flooding, heat waves. . . . It's an indication that the climate is spinning out of control."[26]

Tainted Well Water

All life on earth depends on clean, fresh surface water found in streams, ponds, rivers, and lakes. Groundwater is also extremely important. This water flows through the cracks and spaces below the surface into what are known as aquifers. Around half of all Americans depend on aquifers for their drinking water, and groundwater is used to grow around 65 percent of the nation's food. But climate change is threatening the quality of surface water and groundwater in a number of ways.

The most obvious threat to water quality is exemplified by the problems seen in Vermont. During floods, toxic chemicals such as petroleum products and cleaning agents like bleach and ammonia often escape safe storage, leading to contamination of surface water. Even after a rainstorm ends, floodwaters continue to pose a threat. Pools of stagnant water, which can take months to evaporate, become breeding grounds for disease-carrying mosquitoes and also allow pollutants to seep below the surface into groundwater supplies.

> ### CONSIDER THIS
>
> About one-third of wastewater facilities in the United States would be at risk of flooding if hit by a mega storm.
>
> —First Street Foundation, risk-analysis firm

In addition to toxic chemicals, floodwaters contain raw sewage. This pollutant carries high levels of bacteria and pathogens such as E. coli and salmonella. In 2022, after record-setting rainstorms swamped the Midwest, health department worker Stefanie

Floodwaters and Sewage

Few people think about what happens to their wastewater when they flush their toilets. Those who live in cities and suburbs simply assume that their municipal wastewater plants will handle the sewage and return the purified water to local waterways. And that is what happens in normal weather. But during excessive rainstorms, wastewater treatment plants are often the first facilities to flood. These plants are usually built at the lowest point in a community, near the rivers where they discharge clean, treated water. During the torrential downpours that hit Vermont in 2023, rising floodwaters tore through wastewater treatment plants across the state. Buildings, sewer pipes, and other infrastructure were damaged or destroyed. The rising waters overwhelmed tanks holding millions of gallons of raw sewage, allowing the sewage to wash into rivers and lakes.

The situation in Vermont is not isolated. Most of the wastewater treatment plants in North America were built in the twentieth century. And these outdated facilities are extremely expensive to replace, according to water expert Sri Vedachalam. He says, "Wastewater systems are not designed for this changing climate. They were designed for an older climate that probably doesn't exist anymore. . . . [And] the hundreds of millions of dollars needed to rebuild one can equal several times a town's annual budget."

Quoted in Suman Naishadham et al., "Rising Flood Risks Threaten Many Water and Sewage Treatment Plants Across the US," ABC News, August 10, 2023. https://abcnews.go.com.

Johnson and her family could not drink the water on her farm in western Illinois for two months. The muddy brown floodwaters that poured into Johnson's well tested positive for E. coli bacteria, which can cause severe intestinal disease. "I was pretty strict with the kids," says Johnson. "I'd pour bottled water on their toothbrushes. . . . Luckily, none of us became ill."[27]

The EPA says that around 53 million US residents draw their water from private wells, which are fed by groundwater. Some live in rural areas, while others reside in subdivisions that are built beyond the reach of municipal water treatment systems. After heavy rainfalls and flooding, those who rely on wells might find themselves drinking contaminated water. When Hurricane Ida hit Mississippi in 2021, hundreds of wells were found to contain three times the normal level of E. coli. As environmental engineer Kelsey Pieper points out, the threat to wells and groundwater is growing as climate change causes stronger storms. "Areas that hadn't been impacted are now. New areas are getting flooded. We know the environment is shifting and we're playing catch-up, trying to increase awareness."[28]

Nutrient Pollution

Raw sewage is only one type of contaminant transported into groundwater during heavy rains and floods. Another threat comes from agricultural fertilizers, which contain large quantities of chemicals such as nitrogen and phosphorus. Nitrogen and phosphorus provide essential nutrients to corn, soybeans, and other crops. But too much of a good thing can be bad for the environment. When chemical fertilizers wash into lakes and rivers during rainstorms, they allow algae to grow and multiply into giant masses called algae blooms. This lowers water quality by what is called nutrient pollution. Algae are naturally occurring microscopic organisms, sometimes referred to as pond scum. Algae naturally float on the surface of freshwater. But algae blooms consume excessive amounts of oxygen in water and prevent sunlight from reaching aquatic plants. This suffocates fish and upsets the natural balance of freshwater ecosystems.

CONSIDER THIS

Every year around 1.3 million Americans suffer from acute gastrointestinal illness caused by drinking contaminated well water.

—Heather Murphy, epidemiologist

A 2022 study published by *Environmental Research Letters* found that nutrient pollution is increasing as climate change makes rain more common in the winter. This is especially true in places like the Midwest, where snowstorms are giving way to winter rainstorms. When agricultural fields are covered with snow, the frozen soil holds farm chemicals in place. But when the soil is warmer, researchers have found, natural microbial activity increases levels of nitrogen. This washes into groundwater and other freshwater sources during winter rainstorms.

Algae blooms consume excessive amounts of oxygen, which suffocates and kills fish in large numbers.

According to the study, this extra nutrient pollution is expected to lower groundwater quality in around 40 percent of the United States. Carol Adair, a University of Vermont researcher and co-author of the report, explains the findings: "The idea of winter nutrient pollution is new, because it's a relatively recent impact of climate change with the potential to cause significant problems for people and the environment. . . . We are clearly seeing much larger amounts of cloudy water and sediment traveling through U.S. watersheds in winter."[29]

Rising Groundwater

Contaminated floodwater is one of the most obvious sources of water pollution, but it is not the only one. Rising sea levels resulting from climate change are also contributing to groundwater pollution. Sea levels are rising throughout the world as warm temperatures melt mountain glaciers and massive ice fields in Greenland, Antarctica, and the Arctic. Sea levels have already increased about 9 inches (23 cm) on average since the late nineteenth century. Climate scientists expect sea levels to continue to rise around the world by as much as 3 feet (91 cm) by 2100.

It is well understood that rising sea levels are responsible for increased flooding in coastal regions, especially during hurricanes. But rising sea levels are causing pollution problems for people who live miles from the ocean. As seas expand, excess water flows not only onto the land but also into underground aquifers. The inflow of seawater through the cracks between rocks, sand, and soil beneath the earth is pushing groundwater up to the surface in some places. This is causing problems for rural residents whose homes are not connected to municipal wastewater treatment facilities. These people rely on septic systems, underground containers that hold sewage from toilets and wastewater from sinks and showers.

Drugs Drift into Waterways

When flooding occurs, it is expected that farm chemicals and petroleum products will be detected in waterways. But floodwaters also carry unexpected pollutants from other sources that can be almost as harmful. This problem was illustrated in 2021 after catastrophic flooding swamped southern British Columbia, Canada. The environmental group Raincoast Conservation Foundation discovered over 260 contaminants in water samples taken from Sumas Lake in Abbotsford. Some chemicals came from common household products like toothpaste, cosmetics, and cleaners that washed into the lake. The foundation also detected pharmaceutical drugs, including antidepressants, amphetamines, painkillers, and birth control pills. Small portions of these drugs pass through the human body and are flushed into sewer systems.

When wastewater treatment plants are overwhelmed by floods, the drugs end up in waterways. This pharmaceutical pollution can negatively affect aquatic creatures and ecosystems. And the problem is not confined to a single lake in Canada. Pharmaceutical ingredients have been found in high concentrations in waterways in the United States, Europe, Asia, Africa, and elsewhere. As climate change increases the number and intensity of floods, medicine and other consumer chemicals will wind up in water that is essential to all living creatures.

In Beauford County, South Carolina, raw sewage from septic systems is being pushed to the surface by groundwater expansion blamed on rising sea levels. This stinking, polluted waste oozes into people's yards above their buried septic tanks. When it rains, the sewage is washed into rivers, lakes, and the ocean. And the problem is not isolated to South Carolina. Around one in five US households is connected to a septic system, and rising groundwater is infiltrating these systems in Virginia, Florida, and elsewhere.

Power Plant Waste Products

Rising sea levels can force groundwater to the surface even when it is not raining. A problem called groundwater flooding occurs during intense rainstorms that dump heavy precipitation over a short period. The excess water percolates into the soil and overwhelms the aquifers below. This phenomenon causes pools of water to remain on the surface, rather than seep into the ground. While groundwater flooding can be relatively harmless, it can seriously lower water quality when it overwhelms toxic waste storage facilities called coal ash ponds. This is the situation in the Midwest, where the number of extreme rainstorms has doubled in the past century.

Coal ash is a by-product of coal-fired power plants. There are 220 coal-fired power plants in the United States, and they generate around 110 million tons (100 million metric tonnes) of coal ash annually. Most of it is stored in 735 open coal ash ponds around the country. The ashes of burned coal contain extremely toxic compounds, including mercury, lead, arsenic, and cadmium. Exposure to coal ash can cause dizziness, nausea, vomiting, shortness of breath, liver and kidney damage, and a variety of cancers.

Coal ash ponds are often unlined; they do not contain plastic or concrete barriers that prevent toxins from seeping into groundwater. During groundwater flooding events, toxins float to the surface in areas around coal ash ponds. These hazardous chemicals then wash into waterways. The Vermilion Power Station, located on the Vermilion River near Danville in central Illinois, illustrates the problem. When the coal-fired power plant closed in 2011, over

Toxins from coal ash ponds can seep into groundwater or wash into waterways during flood events. This photo shows an ash pond that leaked into the Dan River, in Eden, North Carolina.

3 million cubic yards (2.3 million cu. m) of coal ash remained on the site in three unlined ponds. During rainstorms the banks of the Vermilion River turn bright orange and take on an oily sheen from the toxins that flood out of the groundwater. In 2023 Dynegy, the company that owns the power plant, agreed to move the coal ash to a lined landfill after losing a lawsuit by a local environmental group. But there are at least 163 coal ash ponds in Illinois, Missouri, Iowa, and Indiana where groundwater flooding is a problem.

Widespread damage caused by rain and floods attracts a lot of attention. But slow-moving crises like groundwater flooding and pollution remain urgent issues that need to be addressed. Marine researcher Molly Mitchell believes it is vital to study these problems and educate the public. She says, "I think sometimes when we talk about issues related to changing environments, it can seem overwhelming or depressing. But I really think the important thing is that when we have good information about the future, we make better decisions."[30]

CHAPTER FOUR

Altered Oceans

In 2023 massive amounts of seaweed blanketed beaches in Florida. The slimy brown sargassum seaweed was part of a free-floating blob that was 5,000 miles (8,047 km) long and 300 miles (483 km) wide. The island of seaweed stretched from Africa to the Gulf of Mexico. Seaweed blooms are not unusual in the region, and sargassum plays a vital role in ocean ecosystems. But some of the piles on Florida beaches were 5 feet (1.5 m) deep. Not only did the seaweed make the beaches impassible, the decaying mess released hydrogen sulfide, which smells like rotten eggs.

Scientists said the seaweed bloom was the largest ever recorded and the first that could be detected from space by satellites. The bloom was able to reach its record-breaking size thanks to the combined effects of climate change and water pollution.

Sargassum seaweed is a type of algae. Like other algae, sargassum thrives by converting sunlight and carbon dioxide into a plantlike biomass. The burning of fossil fuels is increasing the amount of carbon dioxide in the atmosphere. The ocean is known as a carbon sink because it absorbs about one-third of the human-created CO_2 in the air. Algae needs CO_2 to survive, but the higher levels in the environment allow sargassum to grow out of control.

Agricultural runoff that contains nitrogen fertilizer further encourages gargantuan algae blooms that lower ocean water quality. In 2021 algae specialist and research professor Brian Lapointe found that nitrogen levels in seaweed were 35 percent higher compared to seaweed collected in 1980. Lapointe says, "It's almost like sargassum is a barometer for how global nitrogen levels are changing." Sargassum seaweed would not pose a threat if climate change were not warming waters, increasing CO_2 levels, and feeding huge blooms in the ocean. But Lapointe does not expect the situation to change any time soon: "I remember seeing *The Blob* [a 1988 horror] movie when I was a kid and it scared . . . [me]. This blob of seaweed is scarier. It's the real deal."[31]

Plastic Ocean Pollution

Seaweed can be used for food, natural fertilizer, and even nonpolluting biofuel. But as the algae floats across the sea, it absorbs pollutants, including heavy metals like arsenic. Researchers have also found another type of contaminant mixed in with the seaweed—plastic debris. Every year more than 12 million tons (11 million metric tonnes) of plastic enters the ocean, according to the environmental group Ocean Conservancy. This adds to the 220 million tons (200 metric tonnes) of plastic garbage that is already circulating in the sea. This trash includes countless plastic water bottles, straws, bags, and almost every consumer product. And it is impacting ocean ecosystems throughout the world.

Seaweed covers the beach in Fort Lauderdale, Florida, in 2023, a year in which massive amounts of sargassum seaweed blanketed Florida beaches.

Climate change is not responsible for plastic pollution in the ocean, but warming global temperatures are adding an extra threat. Researchers have found an extremely aggressive type of vibrio bacteria that has adapted to living on plastic trash in hotter ocean waters. Vibrio bacteria can attach itself to even the tiniest pieces of plastic, known as microplastics. Microplastics form when plastic products break down into fragments that are less than 5 millimeters in diameter, or about one-third the size of a dime. If a person has an open cut on his or her foot and walks through plastic-contaminated sargassum on a beach, the cut can become infected with vibrio. This can cause serious illnesses, including cholera and leaky gut syndrome, which leads to several other systemic diseases. The Centers for Disease Control and Prevention says vibrio bacteria is responsible for an estimated eighty thousand illnesses and one hundred deaths in the United States every year.

> ## CONSIDER THIS
>
> The oceans contain 99 percent of all habitat on earth.
>
> —Gene Feldman, oceanographer

Breaking the Biological Carbon Pump

Seaweed is part of a complex web of biodiversity, a term that describes the diverse array of plant, animal, algae, fungi, and microbe species in aquatic and land environments. Microscopic algae called phytoplankton provide a foundation for biodiversity in the ocean. Phytoplankton have evolved into a large number of species that provide a foundation for the aquatic food chain that sustains all life in the ocean.

Microscopic animals called zooplankton work with phytoplankton to remove CO_2 from the air. This process is called the biological carbon pump. The biological carbon pump sequesters (removes and stores) approximately 13.2 billion tons (12 billion metric tonnes) of CO_2 annually. Without this vital function, the amount of CO_2 in the air would be around 50 percent higher than it is now and would likely result in mass extinctions.

The biological carbon pump begins when phytoplankton absorb carbon dioxide from the surface of the ocean. Like plants on land, the phytoplankton use sunlight to convert CO_2 into energy through the process of photosynthesis. The biological carbon pump process continues as zooplankton eat phytoplankton. The CO_2 is transferred to the zooplankton, which excrete it in fecal pellets that sink to the bottom of the ocean. The CO_2 in zooplankton feces combines with minerals to become rocks on the seafloor. This prevents the chemical from returning to the atmosphere. As marine ecologist Clara Manno explains, "The biological carbon pump helps to keep the planet healthy. It helps the mitigation of climate change."[32]

Researchers have found that microplastics are interfering with the biological carbon pump, which is lowering the water quality in the ocean. Zooplankton are unintentionally ingesting plastic fragments that are just one-millionth of a millimeter in size—a tiny fraction of the width of a human hair. The particles, also known

Microplastics in the Ocean

Plastic is made from oil, and plastic production contributes to climate change. In addition to increasing the amount of carbon dioxide pollution in the atmosphere, plastic is lowering water quality in the ocean. When plastic bags, water bottles, lawn chairs, and other garbage float in the ocean, the trash breaks down into basic chemicals. This process, called photodegradation, is caused by sunlight interacting with seawater. Depending on the type of plastic, photodegradation can take from a few months to five hundred years. Photodegradation turns plastic objects into microplastics. The basic elements of microplastics are called polymers. Unlike plants and animals, the synthetic molecules of polymers are indestructible to microorganisms that normally break down organic matter.

By the middle of the twenty-first century, three times more plastic will be produced throughout the world than was made in 2016. According to researchers at the World Economic Forum, "The ocean is expected to contain 1 ton of plastic for every 3 tons of fish by 2025, and by 2050, more plastics than fish (by weight)."

Len Neufeld et al., "The New Plastics Economy: Rethinking the Future of Plastics," World Economic Forum, 2016. www3.weforum.org.

Microplastics, as shown here, are interfering with the biological carbon pump, which is lowering water quality in the ocean.

as nanoplastics, mix with zooplankton fecal pellets. Since plastic floats, it causes the feces to sink much more slowly to the ocean floor. According to a study by the Plymouth Marine Laboratory in the United Kingdom, the pellets with nanoplastics are sinking at less than half the normal speed. This means zooplankton fecal pellets spend up to three extra days drifting through ocean waters. According to marine ecologist Matthew Cole, who led the Plymouth study, this makes the fecal pellets more vulnerable to breaking or being eaten by ocean creatures. When that happens, less CO_2 reaches the ocean floor to be sequestered.

Troubles with the biological carbon pump are compounded as nanoplastics reduce the number of zooplankton in the sea. Plastic pollution is toxic to zooplankton. Nanoparticles clog the digestive systems of the tiny creatures, preventing them from eating enough food. Cole studied a common type of zooplankton called copepods. He found that plastic ingestion reduced the copepod growth rate by up to 45 percent, and the creatures produced smaller eggs that were less likely to hatch. Copepods that consumed nanoplastics lived shorter-than-normal lives. With fewer healthy zooplankton, the important role that these microscopic creatures play in cleaning the oceans and the atmosphere will continue to diminish.

Acid Oceans

Zooplankton are facing another threat as their natural food source is overwhelmed by the sheer volume of CO_2 being absorbed by the ocean. When CO_2 dissolves in seawater, a chemical called carbonic acid is produced. This chemical reaction has caused the world's oceans to become around 30 percent more acidic than they were during the eighteenth century.

Ocean acidification is threatening sea creatures that build their shells or skeletons from calcium carbonate. These marine species, known as calcifying organisms, include coral, phytoplankton, krill, and marine invertebrates such as clams, mollusks, oysters, crabs, and sea snails. In addition to dissolving calcium, acid reduces the amount of calcium in seawater, making it more difficult for calcifying organisms to grow and thrive.

Ocean acidification is also damaging coral reefs—colonies of living coral that are held together by calcium carbonate. Coral reefs grow in shallow, clear water where sunlight is abundant. They are sometimes referred to as rain forests of the sea because of their incredible biodiversity. While coral reefs occupy less than 0.1 percent of the total area of the ocean, they provide habitat to around 25 percent of all marine species. Large numbers of fish species, sponges, mollusks, sea worms, starfish, and sea urchins depend on coral reefs for survival.

Thermal Pollution

Coral reefs and the biodiversity they support face another threat. The oceans absorb 90 percent of the excess heat generated by climate change, according to the National Oceanic and Atmospheric Administration (NOAA). In the summer of 2023, this caused average sea surface temperatures to rise 1.85°F (1°C) higher than average in the North Atlantic, the region of the Atlantic Ocean north of the equator. Some spots in the North Atlantic spiked by as much as 5.4°F (3°C). The seawater near Everglades National Park in Florida topped 101°F (38.3°C), about the same temperature as a hot tub. Climate scientist Daniel Swain put these readings in perspective: "The North Atlantic is record-shatteringly warm right now. There has never been any day in observed history where the entire North Atlantic has been nearly as warm as it is right now, at any time of year."[33]

Most people do not think of warm water as harmful, but scientists refer to abnormal ocean heat as thermal pollution. As energy engineer James G. Speight explains, "Thermal pollution is the degradation of water quality by any process that changes the ambient water temperature."[34] Coral, fish, and other aquatic creatures that have adapted to specific ocean temperature ranges are killed by spikes in water temperature. Known as thermal shock, it

Acid in the Ocean

Ocean acidification is discussed in terms of the pH value of the water; pH stands for "potential of hydrogen." This value represents the number of hydrogen atoms in a substance on a numeric scale of 1 to 14 that specifies whether a liquid is acidic, neutral, or alkaline. Liquids with low pH values, around 1 or 2, are highly acidic; vinegar has a pH of 2.4. Distilled water is neutral with a pH of 7. A high pH value of 12 or 13 indicates a solution is highly alkaline. Coral and the shells of oysters, mussels, and other mollusks are made from calcium carbonate, a relatively alkaline substance with a pH of 9.9.

For millions of years the oceans maintained a pH of 8.2. But since the start of the Industrial Revolution about 250 years ago, the oceans have been absorbing acidic carbon dioxide with a pH of 5.6. This has reduced the pH of the ocean to 8.1. Although a reduction from 8.2 to 8.1 pH might not sound like much, one pH point represents a tenfold change in acidity. Today the ocean is approximately 30 percent more acidic than it was during the eighteenth century—and seawater has not been this acidic in 14 million years. While the ocean is scrubbing CO_2 from the atmosphere, the acidification is impairing the growth rate and survival of critical ocean species, including phytoplankton, krill, coral, and mollusks.

is detrimental to the biodiversity of the ocean. "If you have several species that are being impacted at the same time by an increase in temperature, there's going to be a general collapse of the whole ecosystem,"[35] says Professor Mariana Fuentes.

The Heat Blob

Thermal pollution is driving a major increase in marine heat waves, extended periods of above-average ocean water temperatures. According to NOAA, the number of marine heat waves has increased by 50 percent since 2010. And in August 2023, 48 percent of the world's oceans were in the midst of a heat wave.

Marine heat waves lower ocean water quality from the ocean surface to the seafloor. The damage to ecosystems is exemplified by one of the most studied marine heat waves, known as the Blob. From 2014 through 2016, a large mass of warm water raised ocean temperatures around 9°F (5°C) above average along the West Coast of North America. Researchers called this massive area of warm water "the Blob" because it appeared as a giant red blob on ocean surface temperature maps. When the Blob returned three years later, it was given a technical name—the Northeast Pacific Marine Heat Wave of 2019.

> ## CONSIDER THIS
>
> Burning fossil fuels has made the oceans more acidic than they have been in the past 14 million years.
>
> —Sindia Sosdian, marine biochemist

The first appearance of the Blob caused a disease called sea star wasting syndrome, which wiped out millions of starfish. The hardest-hit species, the sunflower sea star, is one of the most colorful starfish in the ocean. Not only pleasing to the eye, the sunflower sea star also plays a key role in the kelp forest ecosystem. Kelp is a type of algae that grows into dense ocean "forests" along one-quarter of all coastlines on earth, and some species grow to a height of more than 175 feet (53 m). Kelp forests are food-generating ecosystems that have been supporting human populations for hundreds of thousands of years. They provide

The sunflower sea star, shown here, plays a key role in the kelp forest ecosystem. It has been devastated by sea star wasting syndrome, caused by rising ocean temperatures.

breeding grounds for fish, shellfish, and other seafood, and dried seaweed is an important addition to Chinese, Korean, and Japanese cuisines. In addition to providing a habitat for an immense number of creatures, kelp forests sequester around twenty times more CO_2 than do forests on land. This helps temper ocean acidification. But when one piece of the web of life is removed, the entire kelp forest ecosystem is impacted.

The sea star was the only predator of the purple sea urchin, which feeds on kelp. The disappearance of the sea stars created a sea urchin population boom. In 2019 around 350 million purple sea urchins were counted along a single reef in Oregon, a 10,000 percent increase since 2014. By 2021 the spiny purple urchins created what were called urchin barrens—vast areas of denuded seafloor where kelp forests once thrived. In Northern California 95 percent of the coastal kelp forests were devoured by purple sea urchins.

In addition to threatening biodiversity, the urchin invasion had a devastating impact on the seafood industry. The closure of cod, clam, abalone, and Dungeness crab fisheries resulted in a loss of around $366 million in Washington, Oregon, and California, according to a 2021 study by NOAA.

All life on earth came from the sea, and the well-being of humanity—and countless other species—depends on healthy oceans. But when climate change interacts with the by-products of modern society, like microplastics and fertilizers, the ability of the ocean to cleanse itself and the atmosphere is disrupted. In this way even pollution that is not directly related to climate change interacts with warming temperatures to lower the quality of seawater. Society needs to address these problems and reduce the threats to ensure not only the well-being of the oceans but the health of humanity in the years to come.

> ## CONSIDER THIS
>
> The Great Barrier Reef in Australia provides habitat for four hundred types of coral, fifteen hundred species of fish, and four thousand types of mollusks.
>
> —United Nations Educational, Scientific and Cultural Organization

CHAPTER FIVE

Solutions to Climate Pollution

In 2023, a year marked by smoke-blackened skies and devastating downpours, a group of young people in Montana won a landmark environmental lawsuit. The lawsuit, filed against the state of Montana, was brought by plaintiffs ranging in age from five to twenty-two. The suit challenged a Montana law that prevented state officials from considering the impact of climate change when granting permits for energy projects. At the time the lawsuit was filed, Montana was the nation's fifth-largest coal producer and twelfth-largest producer of oil. The state relied on coal-fired power plants to produce around one-third of its electricity.

The Montana state constitution guarantees "the right to a clean and healthful environment . . . for present and future generations."[36] Acknowledging this wording, Judge Kathy Seeley ruled in favor of the young people. Seeley wrote that the state violated its own constitution when approving fossil fuel projects because it failed to consider the effects of climate change: "Montana's emissions and climate change have been proven to be a substantial factor in causing . . . harm and injury"[37] to the plaintiffs. Immediately after the ruling, the state of Montana announced it would appeal the decision.

The case, known as *Held v. Montana*, was historic in that it was the first youth-led climate lawsuit to go to trial in the United States. Environmental law expert Michael Gerrard says, "I think this is the strongest decision on climate change ever issued by any court. . . . The court issued a 103-page decision that found that fossil fuel use is the principal cause of climate change, which is in turn causing serious health and environmental impacts that will continue to get worse."[38] Legal experts believe that Seeley's decision helps establish the legal precedent that governments have a duty to protect their citizens from climate change. The Global Climate Change Litigation Database expects the ruling to provide a legal road map for other judges presiding over some of the seven hundred climate-related lawsuits that have been filed worldwide.

Helping File Lawsuits

The plaintiffs in the Montana lawsuit were guided through the complex court process by a nonprofit group called Our Children's Trust. The group was founded by environmental attorney Julia Olson to help young people file lawsuits against government policies that promote fossil fuels. As Olson said after the ruling, "As fires rage in the West, fueled by fossil fuel pollution, today's ruling in Montana is a game-changer that marks a turning point in this generation's efforts to save the planet from the devastating effects of human-caused climate chaos."[39]

Environmental science student Rikki Held was the lead plaintiff in the lawsuit. Held grew up on a ranch near the small town of Broadus, Montana. Like many others, her family has suffered through extreme droughts, floods, and wildfires fueled by climate change. In 2022 there were twenty-five wildfires within 50 miles (80.5 km) of her home, leaving Held's family without electricity for more than a month.

Held and the other plaintiffs believe they represent Montanans under age twenty who are facing an uncertain future due to climate change. As Held says, "Climate change affects everyone, but young people are disproportionately affected. . . . Young people will be exposed longer to the negative effects of climate change, such as air and water pollution and extreme heat."[40]

Plaintiffs in the landmark Held v. Montana *climate change lawsuit walk to the Lewis and Clark County Courthouse in Helena during their trial.*

Cleansing the Air

Climate change lawsuits are not the only way to bring about change. Some states are taking active measures on their own in an effort to reduce the harms caused by fossil fuel consumption. In 2022 California enacted a measure called the California Climate Commitment. The state committed to cutting air pollution by more than 70 percent by 2045 while slashing greenhouse gas emissions by 85 percent. The measure also pledges to cut the state's fossil fuel use by 95 percent. As journalist Tasmiha Khan writes, "Reducing emissions could help prevent millions of premature deaths brought on by air pollution during the following century. Reducing carbon emissions not only improves overall air quality and safeguards human health—it is absolutely essential in the fight against climate change."[41]

Almost all climate scientists agree that the most obvious way to fight both air pollution and climate change is to stop burning fossil fuels. But that would not remove the gigatons of excessive

CO_2 already in the atmosphere. Scientists say it could take hundreds of years for carbon dioxide concentrations to return to natural levels. This is prompting researchers to seek ways to scrub CO_2 from the air. The technology, known as carbon capture, is still in the early stages of development.

> ## CONSIDER THIS
>
> Earth's forests absorb 8.3 billion tons (7.5 billion metric tonnes) of carbon dioxide annually, about one-third of annual global emissions.
>
> —World Resources Institute

A Swiss company called Climeworks is focusing on a CO_2 removal technology called direct air capture (DAC). Climeworks opened two DAC plants in Iceland, the first in 2021 and a second, larger plant in 2022. Each facility uses giant fans to draw in air from the atmosphere. The air crosses chemically treated filters that trap CO_2 molecules. High heat is applied to the filters, which causes them to release the trapped carbon dioxide. The CO_2 is piped underground, where it is trapped in porous rock formations. The company's larger plant annually removes the

Using Artificial Intelligence to Curb Wildfires

Wildfires have been blamed for a massive spike in air pollution in recent years. The best way to solve that problem is to stop fires before they grow out of control. In 2023 California turned to artificial intelligence (AI) to help accomplish that goal. The California Department of Forestry and Fire Protection is relying on AI to monitor the more than one thousand high-definition cameras with infrared night vision that are located in strategic areas throughout the state to watch for signs of fire.

AI can detect smoke from small fires and alert firefighters immediately. In July 2023 battalion chief Scott Slumpff was awakened at 3:00 a.m. by the AI system, which detected a 10-by-10-foot (3 by 3 m) fire east of San Diego. Firefighters were immediately dispatched, and brought the fire under control. Without the alert, Slumpff says, "we wouldn't have even known about the fire until the next morning. . . . We probably would have been looking at hundreds of acres rather than a small spot." In its first two months of use, the AI system detected seventy-seven unreported fires.

Quoted in Haley Smith, "As California Fires Worsen, Can AI Come to the Rescue?," *Los Angeles Times*, August 24, 2023. www.latimes.com.

CONSIDER THIS

In 2023 around 130 direct air capture plants, which remove CO_2 from the atmosphere, were in various stages of development around the world.

—International Energy Agency

equivalent of the emissions produced by five thousand homes.

Other companies are also getting involved in direct air capture. In 2022, nineteen DAC plants were in operation worldwide. The International Energy Agency says many more such plants are needed. For direct air capture to have any real effect, the agency says, thirty-two large-scale plants need to be built every year before 2050. Some of the world's biggest companies are betting that direct air capture and storage can save the planet. Microsoft, United Airlines, and Amazon have invested billions of dollars in developing and improving the technology. Steve Oldham, chief executive officer of a Canadian DAC company called Carbon Engineering, believes that the technology can be scaled up to remove some

This photo shows Climeworks direct air capture fans on the roof of a garbage incinerator outside of Zurich, Switzerland.

of the billions of tons of CO_2 produced every year: "We have a climate change problem and it's caused by an excess of CO_2. With DAC," he says, "you can remove any emission, anywhere, from any moment in time. It's a very powerful tool to have."[42]

Cleaning Up the Ocean

As DAC companies work to improve air quality, George Waldbusser is working to improve ocean water quality. Waldbusser is a professor of ocean ecology and biogeochemistry at Oregon State University. In the 2010s he was contacted by owners of failing West Coast oyster hatcheries. These hatcheries sell three-week-old oysters, called seeds, to seafood farmers who "plant" them in bays and estuaries. The oyster seeds are no bigger than a strand of hair, but when they grow into full-size oysters, the farmers can sell them to consumers. However, the oyster seeds were dying off due to rising ocean acid levels caused by carbon dioxide emissions. The acidification prevented baby oysters from naturally producing shells as they grow.

Waldbusser calls ocean acidification the evil twin of climate change. "I think of it as the heartburn of the sea," he says. "And it was threatening thousands of jobs in rural coastal communities. Fortunately, it also presented an opportunity to try something new: We prescribed an antacid."[43] Waldbusser helped set up a system in a small Oregon bay that lowered ocean acidity by adding soda ash (sodium carbonate) to the water. The technique is called ocean alkalinity enhancement (OAE) because soda ash, with a pH of around 11.6, is extremely alkaline.

After the OAE project was initiated at the Whiskey Creek Shellfish Hatchery in 2010, the facility was able to produce billions of healthy oyster seeds. The techniques pioneered at the hatchery are now being used around the world. Researchers at the National Academy of Sciences are seeking ways to reduce CO_2 levels in the ocean on a larger scale.

Lowering Temperatures on the Ground

Dumping alkaline soda ash into the ocean helps lower acid levels. This type of human manipulation of the earth's large-scale natural systems is referred to as geoengineering or climate intervention. And as water and air quality continue to plummet due to climate change, numerous experimental geoengineering projects are being initiated with the hope that some will be able to contain the damage.

One method of climate intervention is called solar aerosol injection. Solar aerosol injection involves using balloons, airplanes, and even rockets to spread sulfuric acid particles, or sulfate aerosols, in the stratosphere. In this atmospheric layer, located 7 to 31 miles (11.3 to 50 km) above the earth's surface, the sulfate aerosols reflect some of the sun's heat back into space. In effect, this creates a thin sunshade that lowers ground temperatures and limits the number of smog-producing heat domes that lower air quality.

> ## CONSIDER THIS
>
> Two pounds (907 g) of sulfur in the atmosphere can offset the warming effects of around 400,000 pounds (181,000 kg) of carbon dioxide.
>
> —Council on Foreign Affairs

There are several benefits to solar aerosol injection. The process could be started immediately, and at $2.5 billion a year, it is relatively cheap considering that climate change weather disasters have cost the United States more than $2.4 trillion since 1980, according to NOAA. However, there are unknown hazards. The stratosphere contains a layer of ozone that prevents harmful radiation from hitting the earth. Scientists are unsure whether the release of sulfuric acid high in the stratosphere will harm the ozone layer.

Geoengineering remains controversial. Adding or removing chemicals on a large scale might have unintended consequences. People have already caused massive changes to life-sustaining air and water systems by burning fossil fuels. But as the quality of

Creating Jobs to Fight Climate Change

In 2023 President Joe Biden launched a program to put twenty thousand young Americans to work fighting climate change. The American Climate Corps pays participants to install solar panels, plant trees, strengthen community resistance to climate disasters, and restore waterways harmed by fossil fuel extraction. Biden created the corps after intense lobbying from the youth-led environmental group Sunrise Movement. According to a White House press release:

> The American Climate Corps is a new initiative that will provide the next generation of Americans with job training and service opportunities to work on a wide range of projects that tackle climate change—including restoring coastal wetlands to protect communities from storm surges and flooding, deploying clean energy, managing forests to improve health and prevent catastrophic wildfires, implementing energy efficient solutions to cut energy bills for hardworking families, and more. All American Climate Corps programs will . . . provide pathways to high-quality employment opportunities in the public and private sectors. No prior experience is required for most positions.

White House, "Biden-Harris Administration Launches American Climate Corps to Train Young People in Clean Energy, Conservation, and Climate Resilience Skills, Create Good-Paying Jobs and Tackle the Climate Crisis," September 20, 2023. www.whitehouse.gov.

air and water continues to deteriorate from climate change, calls for climate intervention are getting louder. As the United Nations Environment Programme framed it in 2023, "Should the effects of climate change become broadly perceived to be unbearable, and the political pressure for governments to cool the Earth become intense, [geoengineering] is the only known means available for governments that might feasibly cool the Earth on politically relevant time scales."[44]

Fighting for the Future

Climate change is one of the greatest problems ever faced by humanity. Reversing the effects of a warming planet on air and water requires big, expensive solutions. Only governments—and wealthy corporations—can be expected to roll out solutions on

Activists march through the streets of Midtown Manhattan on September 17, 2023, as part of the March to End Fossil Fuels.

a scale large enough to slow or neutralize global warming. However, there are more than 8 billion people on earth. And individuals can make their voices heard to demand action from corporations, politicians, and government officials.

In September 2023 around seventy-five thousand climate activists from all walks of life gathered in New York City in a protest called the March to End Fossil Fuels. The demonstration was held at the United Nations headquarters, where world leaders were gathering to attend what was called the Climate Ambition Summit. The meeting was held to prod nations into confronting the climate emergencies that were occurring nearly every day.

As the name implies, the March to End Fossil Fuels was focused on confronting the fossil fuel industry. Timothy Q. Donaghy, researcher for the environmental group Greenpeace, explains why this goal is important by listing the multiple problems associated with fossil fuel production:

> Each stage of the fossil fuel life cycle—extraction, processing, transport, and combustion—generates toxic air and water pollution, as well as greenhouse gas (GHGs) emissions that drive the global climate crisis. In the U.S. the public health hazards from air and water pollution, and risks associated with climate change, fall disproportionately on Black, Brown, Indigenous, and poor communities.[45]

Climate scientist Michael Mann attended the March to End Fossil Fuels. Mann is well known for his research proving that average worldwide temperatures have spiked since the 1990s. Despite his research, Mann says that "we're not doomed yet—we have not yet ensured our extinction." He rejects what he calls climate doomism because it causes apathy when people need to keep fighting for a clean, healthy environment. Mann says it is not too late to reduce pollution and CO_2 emissions and hold temperatures down. "We know that the obstacles to keeping warming below catastrophic levels are not yet physical and they're not technological—they're political. . . . We have to get out and vote, and young folks have to get out in huge numbers and vote," Mann says. "If we do that, then we can elect politicians who will act on our behalf, rather than act as a rubber stamp for polluters."[46]

SOURCE NOTES

Introduction: The Planet Is Boiling

1. Joel Charles, "Climate Change Is Killing Us. It's Time to Act," Wisconsin Examiner, July 3, 2023. https://wisconsinexaminer.com.
2. Charles, "Climate Change Is Killing Us."
3. Quoted in Bob Weber, "Wildfires Are 'Hard on Water,' Experts Say," Toronto (ON) Star, August 19, 2018. www.thestar.com.
4. Quoted in Victoria Bisset, "The U.N. Warns 'an Era of Global Boiling' Has Started. What Does That Mean?," Washington Post, July 29, 2023. www.washingtonpost.com.

Chapter One: Gasping for Breath on a Hot Planet

5. Quoted in Ella Roberta Foundation, "Ella's Life and Her Legacy," 2023. https://ellaroberta.org.
6. Quoted in Solcyre Burga, "What to Know About Heat Domes—and How Long They Last," Time, July 27, 2023. https://time.com.
7. World Health Organization, The Health Argument for Climate Action. Geneva: World Health Organization, 2021, p. i.
8. Quoted in Victoria St. Martin, "Tiny Soot Particles from Fossil Fuel Combustion Kill Thousands Annually. Activists Now Want Biden to Impose Tougher Standards," Inside Climate News, November 17, 2022. https://insideclimatenews.org.
9. Niklas Hagelberg, "Air Pollution and Climate Change: Two Sides of the Same Coin," United Nations Environment Programme, April 23, 2019. www.unep.org.
10. Quoted in Clare Nullis, "Air Quality Sinks as Climate Change Accelerates," United Nations Climate Change, September 7, 2022. https://unfccc.int.
11. Quoted in Angely Mercado, "An Unexpected Reason It'll Be Harder to Breathe as Earth Warms," Gizmodo, March 3, 2023. https://gizmodo.com.
12. Quoted in Samantha Harrington, "'In Every Breath We Take': How Climate Change Impacts Pollen Allergies," Yale Climate Connections, April 19, 2023. https://yaleclimateconnections.org.
13. Quoted in Mrinalika Roy, "Poorer Nations Lag Behind Higher-Income Countries in Air Quality Standards: WHO," Reuters, April 2, 2022. www.reuters.com.

Chapter Two: Smoke in the Air

14. Quoted in Leila Fadel and Allison Aubrey, "Heat and Smoke Can Be a Health Hazard—Combined It's Worse," NPR, June 29, 2023. www.npr.org.

15. Amy D. Lykins et al., "Australian Youth Mental Health and Climate Change Concern After the Black Summer Bushfires," National Library of Medicine, April 28, 2023. www.ncbi.nlm.nih.gov.
16. Quoted in Tony Briscoe, "Study Ties Dementia Risk to Pollution Exposure," *Los Angeles Times*, August 31, 2023. https://edition.pagesuite.com.
17. Quoted in Joshua Partlow et al., "The Toxic Aftermath of the Maui Fires Could Last for Years," *Washington Post*, August 17, 2023. www.washingtonpost.com.
18. Quoted in Briscoe, "Study Ties Dementia Risk to Pollution Exposure."
19. Quoted in Gina Jiménez, "When Wildfire Smoke Shrouds a City, People of Color Are Most at Risk," *Mother Jones*, June 19, 2023. www.motherjones.com.
20. Quoted in Erika Edwards and Jessica Klingbaum, "Extreme Heat and Wildfire Smoke Can Collide in Deadly Ways," NBC News, July 19, 2023. www.nbcnews.com.
21. Quoted in Edwards and Klingbaum, "Extreme Heat and Wildfire Smoke Can Collide in Deadly Ways."
22. Quoted in Joshua Partlow, "Wildfire Smoke Is Eroding Decades of Air Quality Improvements, Study Finds," *Washington Post*, September 20, 2023. www.washingtonpost.com.
23. Quoted in Jamie Ducharme, "How Wildfire Smoke Affects Wildlife—and Your Pets," *Time*, June 7, 2023. https://time.com.
24. Stephen J. Pyne, "Welcome to the Pyrocene," Grist, August 18, 2021. https://grist.org.

Chapter Three: Watershed Woes

25. Quoted in Abagael Giles and Corey Dockser, "July Flooding Pulled Nutrients, Waste into Vermont's Waters—and Climate Change Is Making It Worse," Vermont Public, August 24, 2023. www.vermontpublic.org.
26. Quoted in Jessica McKenzie, "Everything, Everywhere, All at Once: The Great Floods of 2023," *Bulletin of the Atomic Scientists*, July 27, 2023. https://thebulletin.org.
27. Quoted in Michael Phillis and John Flesher, "Climate-Driven Flooding Poses Well Water Contamination Risks," Associated Press, June 8, 2022. https://apnews.com.
28. Quoted in Phillis and Flesher, "Climate-Driven Flooding Poses Well Water Contamination Risks."
29. Quoted in John McCracken, "Study: Warming Winters Will Thaw Frozen Manure, Further Polluting U.S. Waters," Grist, October 7, 2022. https://grist.org.
30. Quoted in Julia Kane et al., "Rising Groundwater Levels Are Threatening Clean Air and Water Across the Country," Grist, May 29, 2023. https://grist.org.

Chapter Four: Altered Oceans

31. Quoted in Emily Olson, "Meet the Sargassum Belt, a 5,000-Mile-Long Snake of Seaweed Circling Florida," NPR, March 15, 2023. www.npr.org.
32. Quoted in Joseph Winters, "All That Plastic in the Ocean Is a Climate Change Problem, Too," Grist, October 17, 2022. https://grist.org.
33. Quoted in Haley Smith, "Ocean Temperatures Are Off the Charts, and El Niño Is Only Partially to Blame," *Los Angeles Times*, June 13, 2023. www.latimes.com.
34. James G. Speight, "Thermal Pollution," ScienceDirect, 2023. www.sciencedirect.com.
35. Quoted in Joe Hernandez, "With Florida Ocean Temperatures Topping 100, Experts Warn of Damage to Marine Life," NPR, July 26, 2023. www.npr.org.

Chapter Five: Solutions to Climate Pollution

36. Quoted in David Gelles and Mike Baker, "Judge Rules in Favor of Montana Youths in a Landmark Climate Case," *New York Times*, August 14, 2023. www.nytimes.com.
37. Quoted in Kristoffer Tigue, "Montana Youth Sued Their Government over Climate Change and Won. Here's Why That's a Big Deal," Inside Climate News, August 15, 2023. https://insideclimatenews.org.
38. Quoted in Tigue, "Montana Youth Sued Their Government over Climate Change and Won."
39. Quoted in Gelles and Baker, "Judge Rules in Favor of Montana Youths in a Landmark Climate Case."
40. Quoted in United Nations, "'This Is About Our Human Rights:' U.S. Youths Win Landmark Climate Case," August 29, 2023. www.ohchr.org.
41. Tasmiha Khan, "All the Ways to Remove Carbon Emissions from the Air," *Time*, October 27, 2022. https://time.com.
42. Quoted in Frank Swain, "The Device That Reverses CO_2 Emissions," BBC, March 11, 2021. www.bbc.com.
43. George Waldbusser, "Science Has a Prescription for the Ocean's Heartburn. Some Side Effects Are Worth It," Grist, August 2, 2021. https://grist.org.
44. Quoted in Edwin Chen, "We're Far Short of Climate Goals. Get Ready for Plan B," *Los Angeles Times*, September 10, 2023. www.latimes.com.
45. Timothy Q. Donaghy et al., "Fossil Fuel Racism in the United States: How Phasing Out Coal, Oil, and Gas Can Protect Communities," ScienceDirect, 2023. www.sciencedirect.com.
46. Quoted in D.P. Carrington, "'We're Not Doomed Yet': Climate Scientists Michael Mann on Our Last Chance to Save Humanity," *The Guardian* (Manchester, UK), September 30, 2023. www.theguardian.com.

ORGANIZATIONS AND WEBSITES

Center for Earth, Energy & Democracy (CEED)
https://ceed.org
CEED works with grassroots neighborhood groups, scientists, and policy makers to provide solutions to climate change, pollution, and environmental injustice. The group's website provides access to educational resources, workshops, and tool kits for activists.

Climate Change Impacts
www.epa.gov/climateimpacts
This website hosted by the US Environmental Protection Agency focuses on the effects of climate change on air quality, water quality, ecosystems, the food supply, and other sectors. The site provides solutions and links to related resources.

Earth Guardians
www.earthguardians.org
This worldwide environmental association, led by the young indigenous activist Xiuhtezcatl Martinez, works to slow climate change. Its website provides comprehensive information about organizing, training, and taking action that can be of use to student activists working on local or global issues.

Kids Fight Climate Change
www.kidsfightclimatechange.org
Kids Fight Climate Change is a youth-led nonprofit organization with a mission to educate, motivate, and empower students. Its website features educational information, solutions, climate news, and numerous other resources for those who want to take action.

Our Children's Trust
www.ourchildrenstrust.org
This organization, based in Portland, Oregon, helps young environmentalists sue governments for not fulfilling their obligations to fight climate change. Its website features updates from the latest lawsuits, climate science tutorials, and calls to action.

FOR FURTHER RESEARCH

Books

Ann Eriksson, *Urgent Message from a Hot Planet: Navigating the Climate Crisis*. Custer, WA: Orca, 2022.

Stuart A. Kallen, *Extreme Weather and Climate Change: What's the Connection?* San Diego, CA: ReferencePoint, 2021.

Naomi Klein, *How to Change Everything: The Young Human's Guide to Protecting the Planet and Each Other*. New York: Atheneum, 2022.

Greta Thunberg, *No One Is Too Small to Make a Difference*. New York: Penguin, 2019.

David Wallace-Wells, *The Uninhabitable Earth (Adapted for Young Adults): Life After Warming*. New York: Delacorte, 2023.

Internet Sources

Bridgett Ennis, "What It's like to Sue the Government over Climate Change (She Won)," Yale Climate Connections, August 29, 2023. https://yaleclimateconnections.org.

Tasmiha Khan, "All the Ways to Remove Carbon Emissions from the Air," *Time*, October 27, 2022. https://time.com.

Jessica McKenzie, "Everything, Everywhere, All at Once: The Great Floods of 2023," *Bulletin of the Atomic Scientists*, July 27, 2023. https://thebulletin.org.

Angely Mercado, "An Unexpected Reason It'll Be Harder to Breathe as Earth Warms," Gizmodo, March 3, 2023. https://gizmodo.com.

Stephen J. Pyne, "Welcome to the Pyrocene," Grist, August 18, 2021. https://grist.org.

Joseph Winters, "All That Plastic in the Ocean Is a Climate Change Problem, Too," Grist, October 17, 2022. https://grist.org.

INDEX

Note: Boldface page numbers indicate illustrations.

Adair, Carol, 32
aerosols (PM2.5), 9, 14, 52
agricultural fertilizers, 31–32, **32**, 36
air conditioners, 11–12
AirNow, 17
air pollution
  California commitment to reduce, 48
  causes of
    climate change, 8
    desert dust, 13
    released by plants, 13–14
    wildfires, 4, 21
  in feedback loop with climate change, 11
  health problems from, 4, 17–18
    allergies, 15
    asthma and, 7
    Black Americans and, 10
    black carbon and, 9
    BVOCs and, 14
    cancer-causing compounds released
      during wildfires, 20, **20**
    dementia, 22
    emotional and mental, 19
    homelessness and, 23
    low income Americans and, 24
    substance abuse, 19
    susceptibility to, 4
    WHO and, 16
  number of Americans living in areas with bad
    air quality, 6
  See also deaths, premature; specific
    pollutants
algae blooms, 31, **32**, 36
allergies, 15
American Climate Corps, 53
Anderegg, William, 15
anxiety and air pollution, 19
aquifers, 29
artificial intelligence (AI) to curb wildfires, 49
asthma
  air pollution and, 7
  race and, 10
  seasonal allergies and, 15
attention-deficit/hyperactivity disorder and air
  pollution, 19

Biden, Joe, 53

Billings, Paul, 9
biodiversity, 38
biogenic volatile organic compounds (BVOCs),
  13–14
biological carbon pump, 38–40
Black Americans, 10, 23
black carbon (PM2.5)
  climate change and, 10–11
  on glaciers, **11**
  premature deaths from, 7, 9–10
  production of, 7–8, **8**
  size of particles, 9
Black Summer (Australia), 18–19
Blob, the, 43–44
Burke, Marshall, 26

California, 24–25, 48
California Climate Commitment, 48
Camley, David, 27
Canada
  pharmaceutical pollution in, 33
  wildfires in
    air quality in US and, 4, **5**, 17, 22–23, 25
    extent of, 17
    smoke-pocalypse, 21
carbon capture, 49–51, **50**
carbon dioxide (CO_2)
  biological carbon pump, 38–40
  California commitment to reduce, 48
  direct air capture, 49–51, **50**
  generation of electricity and, 11–12
  kelp forests' sequestration of, 44
  as main driver of climate change, 10
  in oceans, 36, 41, 42
  plants growth and, 15
carbonic acid, 41
carbon sinks, 36
Carlson, Gail, 26
Centers for Disease Control and Prevention,
  10, 38
Charles, Joel, 4
children, susceptibility of, to air pollution, 4
China, electricity usage in, 12
Cleveland Clinic, 23
Climate Ambition Summit, 54
climate change
  air pollution and, 8
  black carbon and, 10–11
  carbon dioxide as main driver of, 10
  in feedback loop with bad air quality, 11

fighting
  adding soda ash to oceans, 51, 52
  American Climate Corps, 53
  carbon capture, 49–51, **50**
  commitments to cut air pollution, 48
  environmental lawsuits, 46–47, **48**
  fossil fuel use reduction, 48–49, **54**, 54–55
  ocean alkalinity enhancement, 51
  with solar aerosol injection, 52
  using AI, 49
groundwater pollution and, 31–33
increase in smog with increase in demand for cooling measures, 12
location of neighborhoods of Black and low-income Americans and, 10
oceans and
  acidification of, 41, 42, 51, 52
  increase in temperature of, 41–45
  rising levels, 32–33
  thermal shock, 42–43
plants' pollen and, 14–15
seaweed blooms and, 36–37
climate intervention, 51, 52
Climeworks, 49–50, **50**
coal ash pollutants, 34–35, **35**
Cole, Matthew, 40–41
copepods, 40–41
coral reefs, 41, 42–43

deaths, premature
from black carbon, 7, 9–10
increase in, on days with excessive heat and high levels of particulate matter, 24, **25**
from vibrio bacteria, 38
dementia, 22
depression and air pollution, 19
deserts, dust from, 13
direct air capture (DAC), 49–51, **50**
Donaghy, Timothy Q., 54–55
drugs as pollutants, 33

electricity, 11–12
Emelko, Monica, 5
environmental lawsuits, 46–47, **48**
Environmental Research (journal), 31

Falljökull glacier (Iceland), **11**
feedback loops, 11, 12
floods
  groundwater flooding, 34–35, **35**
  hazardous chemical spills and, 27
  pharmaceutical pollution and, 33
  raw sewage in, 29–30
  rising sea levels and, 33
  toxic substances after, 5, 29

in Vermont, 27–28, **28**
Florida, 36, **37**, 42
fossil fuels
  California's commitment to reduce use of, 48
  generation of electricity and, 11–12
  protesting use of, **54**, 54–55
Fuentes, Mariana, 43

geoengineering, 51, 52
Gerrard, Michael, 46–47
Ghebreyesus, Tedros Adhanom, 16
Gleick, Peter, 29
Global Climate Change Litigation Database, 47
Gomez, James, 13, 14
Gonzales, Melissa, 24
groundwater
  agricultural fertilizers and, 31–32, **32**
  climate change and pollution of, 31–33
  flooding, 34–35, **35**
  raw sewage in, after floods, 29–30
  rising sea levels and, 34
Guterres, António, 6

Hagelberg, Niklas, 10–11
Hawaii, 21–22
Health Argument for Climate Action, The (WHO), 9
health problems, from air pollution
  allergies, 15
  asthma and, 7
  Black Americans and, 10
  black carbon, 9
  BVOCs, 14
  cancer-causing compounds released during wildfires, 20, **20**
  dementia, 22
  emotional and mental, 19
  homelessness and, 23
  low income Americans and, 24
  substance abuse, 19
  susceptibility to, 4
  WHO and, 16
heart attacks, 4, **25**
heat domes, 8
Held, Rikki, 47
Held v. Montana, 46–47, **48**
Hochul, Kathy, 22
homelessness and air pollution, 23
"Hotter It Gets, the Hotter It Gets, The" (*Science*), 12
Hurricane Ida (Mississippi), 30

Iceland, **11**, 49
Illinois, 29, 34–35
International Energy Agency, 12, 50

Johnson, Stefanie, 29–30
Journal of the American Heart Association, 4

Kalhan, Ravi, 17–18
kelp forests, 43–44
Kentucky, 29
Khan, Tasmiha, 48
Kissi-Debrah, Ella Roberta, 7, 9
Kissi-Debrah, Rosamund, 7

Lahaina (Maui, Hawaii), 21–22
Lapointe, Brian, 36, 37
League, Katie, 23
low-income Americans, 10, 24

Mann, Michael, 55
Manno, Clara, 39
March to End Fossil Fuels, **54**, 54–55
marine heat waves, 43–44
marine species, 41, 42–43
Maui, Hawaii, 21–22
McDougall Creek wildfire, **18**
microplastics, 38, 39, **40**
Mississippi, 30
Mitchell, Molly, 35
Montana, environmental lawsuit in, 46–47, **48**
Montpellier, Vermont, **28**

nanoplastics, 40
National Academy of Sciences, 14, 51
National Climate Assessment, 28
National Institutes of Health, 6
National Oceanic and Atmospheric
    Administration (NOAA), 41, 45, 52
Natural Resources Defense Council, 12
Nature (journal), 26
New England, 28
    See also specific states
nitrogen dioxide (NO_2)
    generation of electricity and, 11–12
    production of, 7–8, **8**
nitrogen in seaweed, 36–37
Northeast Pacific Marine Heat Wave (2019),
    43–44
nutrient pollutants, 31–32, **32**

ocean alkalinity enhancement (OAE), 51
oceans
    acidification of, 41, 42, 51, 52
    as carbon sinks, 36
    groundwater expansion and rising levels
        of, 34
    increase in temperature of, 41–45
    marine heat waves and, 43–44
    plastic pollution in, 37–38, 39–40
    rising levels of, 32–33

seaweed blooms, 36, **37**
thermal shock and aquatic creatures,
    42–43
oil and plastic, 39
Oldham, Steve, 50–51
Olson, Julia, 47
Our Children's Trust, 47
oyster seeds, 51
ozone
    ground level
        described, 5
        increase in demand for cooling measures
            and increase in, 12
        production of, 8
    solar aerosol injection and, 52

particulate matter
    dementia and, 22
    location of neighborhoods of Black and low-
        income Americans and, 10
    PM2.5
        aerosols, 14, 52
        biogenic volatile organic compounds
            (BVOCs), 13–14
        from wildfires, 21
        premature deaths and, 24, **25**
        production of, 7–8, **8**
        See also black carbon (PM2.5)
pharmaceutical pollution, 33
phytoplankton, 38, 39
Pieper, Kelsey, 30–31
plants
    carbon dioxide and growth of, 15
    increase in temperatures and biogenic
        volatile organic compounds release by,
        13–14
    increase in temperatures and pollen release
        by, 14–15, **15**
plastic
    microplastics, 38, 39, **40**
    pollution in oceans, 37–38, 39–40
    production of, 39
Plymouth Marine Laboratory (United Kingdom),
    40
PM2.5. *See under* particulate matter
pollen, 14–15
polycyclic aromatic hydrocarbons (PAHs), 20
polymers, 39
Pyne, Stephen J., 26
Pyrocene era, 26

race and asthma, 10
rain
    coal ash ponds during, 34–35, **35**
    increase in New England, 28
    nutrient pollution and, 31–32

record-breaking, and flooding in US, 27–28, **28**, 29
Raincoast Conservation Foundation, 33
raw sewage and floods, 29–30
raw sewage and rising sea levels, 34
respiratory failure and air pollution, 7

Sahara (North Africa), dust from, 13
sargassum seaweed, 36–37, **37**
Science (journal), 12
seafood industry, 45, 51
sea stars, 43, **44**
sea urchins, 44–45
seaweed, 36–37, **37**
Seeley, Kathy, 46, 47
sewage plants and floods, 29–30
Slumpff, Scott, 49
smog
  described, 5
  increase in demand for cooling measures and increase in, 12
  production of, 8
smoke-pocalypse, 21
soda ash (sodium carbonate), 51, 52
solar aerosol injections, 52
soot. *See* black carbon (PM2.5)
South Carolina, 34
Speight, James G., 42
substance abuse and air pollution, 19
sunflower sea stars, 43, **44**
Swain, Daniel, 42

Taalas, Petteri, 12
temperatures
  increase in
    average global, 13
    nutrient pollution and, 31–32
    oceans', 41–45
    pollen release by plants and, 14–15, **15**
    release of harmful pollutants into air by plants, 13–14
    premature deaths and high, 24, **25**
    water retention and air, 28
Thakur, Neeta, 23–24
thermal pollution, 41–43
thermal shock, 42–43
transportation, production of particulate matter (soot) by, 7–8, **8**
Trudeau, Justin, 17

United Nations Environment Programme, 53
United States
  groundwater flooding in, 34–35, **35**
  raw sewage and rising sea levels in, 34
  wildfires in, 24–25, 26, 49
  wildfires in Canada and air quality in, 4, **5**,
    17, 22–23, 25
  See also specific states
University of California, Riverside (UCR), 13–14
University of Michigan, 22
University of New England (Australia), 18, 19
University of Southern California, 24
urchin barrens, 45
US Environmental Protection Agency (EPA)
  groundwater wells as source of water, 29–30
  number of Americans living in areas with bad air quality, 6
  production of aromatic hydrocarbons, 20
  time spent indoors, 23

Vecchi, Gabriel A., 8
Vedachalam, Sri, 30
Vermilion Power Station (Illinois), 34–35
Vermont, 27–28, **28**, 30
vibrio bacteria, 38

Waldbusser, George, 51
wastewater treatment plants, 30, 33
water
  contaminated drinking, 6
    nutrient pollutants, 31–32, **32**
    pharmaceutical pollution in, 33
    raw sewage and, 29–30
  stagnant, 29
Whelton, Andrew, 22
Whiskey Creek Shellfish Hatchery, 51
wildfires
  in Australia, 18–19
  in Canada, 4, 5, 17, **18**
    smoke-pocalypse and, 21
    spread of smoke from, 4, 5, **5**, 17, 25
  cancer-causing compounds released during, 20, **20**
  as cause of air pollution, 4
  current state of as Pyrocene era, 26
  health effects of, 17–18
  PM2.5 particulate matter from, 21
  toxic materials remaining after, 4–5
  in US, 24–25, 26, 49
World Economic Forum, 39
World Health Organization (WHO)
  on air pollution as health hazard, 9, 16
  black carbon and, 10
  premature deaths from particulate pollution, 10
World Meteorological Organization (WMO), 12
World Weather Attribution, 6

Zhang, Boya, 20, 22
zooplankton, 38, 39–41